HOME BUYING INSIGHTS

*Conversations With America's Leading
Mortgage and Real Estate Professionals*

HOME BUYING INSIGHTS
Conversations With America's Leading Mortgage and Real Estate Professionals

Featuring:

Marty Bronfman

David Lewis

Jason DuPont

Amanda Madsen

Manny Yaquian

Kevin DelGaudio

Remarkable Press™

Royalties from the retail sales of **"HOME BUYING INSIGHTS: CONVERSATIONS WITH AMERICA'S LEADING MORTGAGE AND REAL ESTATE PROFESSIONALS"** are donated to Global Autism Project:

AUTISM KNOWS NO BORDERS;
FORTUNATELY NEITHER DO WE.®

Global autism project 501(C)3, is a nonprofit organization which provides training to local individuals in evidence-based practice for individuals with autism.

Global autism project believes that every child has the ability to learn and their potential should not be limited by geographical bounds.

The global autism project seeks to eliminate the disparity in service provision seen around the world by providing high-quality training to individuals providing services in their local community. This training is made sustainable through regular training trips and contiguous remote training.

You can learn more about Global Autism Project by visiting **GlobalAutismProject.org**

Home Buying Insights / Mark Imperial —1st ed.

Managing Editor/ Shannon Buritz

ISBN-13: 978-1-7323763-1-1

CONTENTS

A NOTE TO THE READER

Thank you for buying your copy of "HOME BUYING INSIGHTS: Conversations With America's Leading Mortgage and Real Estate Professionals." This book was originally created as a series of live interviews, that's why it reads like a series of conversations, rather than a traditional book that talks at you.

I wanted you to feel as though the participants and I are talking with you, much like a close friend, or relative, and felt that creating the material this way would make it easier for you to grasp the topics and put them to use quickly, rather than wading through hundreds of pages.

So relax, grab a pen and paper, take notes and get ready to learn some fascinating, Home Buying Insights.

Warmest regards,

Mark Imperial
Publisher, Author and Radio Personality

INTRODUCTION

"HOME BUYING INSIGHTS: Conversations With America's Leading Mortgage and Real Estate Professionals" is a collaborative book series featuring leading Mortgage and Real Estate Professionals from across the country.

Remarkable Press™ would like to extend a heartfelt thank you to all participants who took the time to submit their chapter and offer their support in becoming ambassadors for this project.

100% of the royalties from the retail sales of this book will be donated to Global Autism Project. Should you want to make a direct donation, visit their website at: GlobalAutismProject.org

MARTY BRONFMAN

Mortgage Solutions for the Credit Challenged

Conversation with Marty Bronfman

Tell us about how you are helping your clients:

Marty Bronfman: I specialize in helping people with credit challenges. I really spend time working with these clients, helping them get over their financial issues and getting them into a position to buy. Many loan officers will bypass these types of clients and move on to the next. I don't do that. These people have goals and ambitions to purchase a home. Everyone deserves that chance. So, I'm going to work with them for six months, a year, or however long it takes to make their dreams a reality. I've been known to help people overcome extremely difficult credit challenges and get them into a home in a couple of months.

The way that I treat my clients is what sets me apart from other professionals in the industry. The whole premise behind the way I do business is to create an exceptional client experience. Often times when dealing with a loan officer, clients are unimpressed by the lack of communication and lack of understanding when it comes to what the loan officer is trying to convey. In response to this problem, I have prided myself over the years in putting together a client experience that is second to none. This experience touches the client multiple times with easy to understand verbiage and vocabulary. Above and beyond all of that, I am also communicating with all parties that are involved in the loan. I coordinate between the selling agent, the buyer's agent, and the attorneys so everybody understands exactly where we stand which ultimately helps prevent issues down the road.

Are there advantages of funding a home purchase with you using your methods?

Marty Bronfman: Yes. When I speak to any referral partner or people who are sending me business, I make a few guarantees. Number one, all preapprovals are thoroughly vetted and guaranteed. Secondly, you will always know where you stand on the particular loan throughout the entire process. And number three, we will close on time every single time. These simple guarantees result in a stress-free home buying process for every party involved.

What does the overall experience look like for a new client?

Marty Bronfman: As mentioned above, the client experience is what I've spent years developing and refining. So, this is really where I shine. If somebody chooses to work with me and my team, they are going to be well taken care of. I equate it to a situation where you are purchasing from a luxury car dealership versus a standard one. When you walk in, you get concierge service and immediately feel appreciated. I have a similar process. Upon walking into our office, the borrowers are immediately greeted by my assistant or the loan partner who will be assigned to them. I also make sure to meet each customer face to face. From this first encounter, the customer is aware of who they can contact, and it creates a sense of security and trust right from the start. From there, the client is pre-approved and sent back to the real estate agent who referred them during the home buying process. The client is contacted once a week and we ask questions such as "Have you found a home?", "Do you need anything updated?", "How can we help?" When they finally do find the house, the mortgage process begins. After receiving the sales contract, we send out the first gift. These gifts are important because they show our clients how much we value them. Just a small token of our appreciation. Upon closing, they receive a more substantial "housewarming gift" to be put to good use in their new home. If my clients are well informed and feeling valued during the entire home buying process, then I have done my job.

What do you feel are the biggest myths out there when it comes to funding a home purchase?

Marty Bronfman: The biggest myth I come across is that you need perfect credit and a 20% down payment in order to buy a home. This is absolutely not true. It is just one more barrier into home ownership that you can successfully overcome when working with the right loan officer. Every borrower has a unique situation. Without the proper guidance, people often get discouraged and their visions of owning a home become cloudy. I devote the time to each individual, no matter the financial circumstances, in order to get them where they need to be. From low credit scores to bankruptcy situations, I have overcome obstacles with my clients so they can qualify for a home mortgage. This is why it is also very important to have a human loan officer as opposed to an online lender. Online lenders answer generalized questions with generalized answers. A home is the largest purchase of your life and you deserve a person to interact with and guide you through the process.

What are some common misconceptions homebuyers have about funding a home purchase or the mortgage industry in general?

Marty Bronfman: Homebuyers often have the misconception that they need spotless credit in order to fund a home purchase. They believe that things like late credit card payments, collection accounts, or bankruptcies will make it impossible to obtain a mortgage. I always tell my clients that our world is very dynamic, and people lead different lives. But nobody is out there living their life according to FHA or Fannie Mae guidelines. It is important to understand there are many gray areas that we can work within.

What are some of the most common fears about funding their home purchase?

Marty Bronfman: The most common fears that I come across are concerns regarding payment. What will the payment be? Will it be feasible for me to make this payment? I go through an entire demonstration with my clients regarding payment. This outlines their exact payment, what they can save on taxes, and what the appreciation or value of their down payment will be in four, five, seven, and ten years. People also fear whether they will qualify for a home mortgage. I am typically able to quell this fear by devoting my time and energy to make that qualification happen, taking into consideration my clients' particular financial situation and home buying goals.

What other perceived obstacles arise during the loan process and how can these be avoided?

Marty Bronfman: I cannot stress enough the importance of having all your documents in order. Many borrowers misplace documents or are not able to find them at the time of loan application. Keep in mind, we will need 60 days of bank statements. Be sure that your checking account looks as typical as possible, with no large deposits that cannot be explained. If you make $5,000 a month and deposit that into checking on a consistent basis, don't all of a sudden grab the $30,000 tucked under your mattress and deposit that as well. It is crucial to have your assets in order and to make sure all of your documents are clear and legible. To keep it simple...remember the two by five rule. You will need two months of bank statements, two years of tax returns, two years W2s or 1099s, two of your most recent pay stubs, and two forms of identification for a smooth mortgage application process.

What inspired you to help folks fund home purchases?

Marty Bronfman: One thing I have always been passionate about is home ownership. I really owe it to my parents for instilling this passion in me. Both of my parents are Russian immigrants and were exiled in the 1970s, forcing them to come to the United States. In hindsight, this was probably the best thing that could have ever happened to them. They came here and never stopped chasing the "American dream". They both worked and saved enough money to purchase their first home. Being ten years old at the time, I was mature enough to see the joy that home

ownership brought to our family and truly appreciate it. We were able to move from a pretty dicey neighborhood into a great neighborhood and enjoy all the benefits...having a backyard, neighbor friends to play with, and a feeling of security. That experience truly
inspired me to help other people get into homes. And during the past 16 years of my career, I have focused my efforts on clients not considered to be "the perfect borrower." I enjoy helping those with financial obstacles the most, as everyone deserves a fair chance at the remarkable feeling of owning a home.

Can you share a lesson you learned early on, that still impacts how you do business today?

Marty Bronfman: A common mistake made by businesses is to give out false promises and create false hopes. In an effort to ensure this never happens to one of my clients, I do not issue a preapproval letter until I have fully reviewed income, assets, and credit history. I have people who call me and say they have a credit score of 720, $50K in the bank, and an annual income of $150,000. That sounds great but be ready to back it up with proper documentation. I want to help people who can actually be helped, and I want to give my referral partners the same opportunity. Which is why I have changed my methods from taking people at their word at the beginning of my career, and now requiring proof and necessary documentation in order to qualify you for a home loan.

What's the most important thing homebuyers should consider when evaluating a mortgage loan officer?

Marty Bronfman: Always ask about their experience, what their process is like and who they help. Who is your customer? I always ask that question. What type of people do you help? I would expect my loan officer to give me meaningful specifics when providing answers to these questions.

How can someone find out more about Marty Bronfman and how you can help?

Marty Bronfman: I have a pretty prolific social media presence, so you can always look me up on Facebook or Instagram, where you can find me at MartyMortgage. On LinkedIn, you can find me at Marty Bronfman. More traditionally, you can call, email, text, or even send a carrier pigeon. My direct number is 201-655-1571. I look forward to helping you achieve your home buying goals.

MARTY BRONFMAN

Regional Vice President / Branch Manager / Mortgage Loan Originator, NMLS 69143

Over the past 15 years, Marty has assisted more than 3,000 families achieve the American dream of homeownership. Marty possesses an extensive background in the mortgage banking industry. Currently, he is an industry leading Regional Vice President, Branch Manager and a Licensed Mortgage Originator, NMLS 69143. He is an

Ithaca College alumni with a degree in economics and finance. Since entering the mortgage banking industry in 2004, Marty has contributed to the significant success of many large banking institutions, but more importantly, to the growth and development of his team and peers. Through his accomplished career, Marty's passion always remained focused on his clients. Providing an exceptional client experience through education and communication is the institution that defines his business.

Marty has specific knowledge of all available loan programs and underwriting guidelines as well as a complete awareness of compliance, laws and regulations governing the real estate industry. Whether you are currently a homeowner wanting to save on your monthly payment, a first-time home buyer, looking to trade up or renovate, deciding to downsize, or simply wishing for a change, Marty can help. He understands the unique, individual needs of each client, creating a roadmap for your budget, income and savings, as well as your family's needs. The home buying or refinancing process can be daunting and confusing, but you can rest assured that Marty always has the security of you and your family in mind.

Marty will always serve the home financing needs of his community working with select business partners. His role allows him to do what he loves; that is to help families achieve their dream of homeownership and gain financial security. Marty understands the needs of a growing family. He is a proud husband and father of three. Much of his time outside of work is spent with his family and contributing to the community. Marty's goal is to be a lifelong mortgage advisor for you and your family.

WEBSITE: https://crosscountrymortgage.com/Marty-Bronfman/

EMAIL: mbronfman1@gmail.com

LINKEDIN: https://www.linkedin.com/in/marty-bronfman-mortgage-expert-5627304/

FACEBOOK:

https://www.facebook.com/martymortgage/

PHONE: (201) 655-1571

DAVID LEWIS

The Power of Renovation Lending

Conversation with Renovation Lending Expert David Lewis

Tell us about how you are helping your clients:

David Lewis: I have been helping clients in the mortgage space for the past 25 years. In that time frame, I have specialized primarily in renovation lending. Early in my career, I realized that there was an abundance of properties out there that were distressed, but absolutely had potential to be great homes that families could grow and thrive in. I wanted to help people find ways to easily finance and renovate these properties into dream homes. I not only help my clients with home purchase loans, but I enable them to easily finance desired or necessary renovations. It can be very difficult to finance renovations after obtaining a conventional type loan. A renovation loan allows you to purchase and renovate in one simple step!

Are there advantages of funding a home purchase with you using your renovation lending methods?

David Lewis: There are a couple significant advantages when it comes to buying "fixer upper" properties as opposed to building from the ground up or purchasing an existing property. First of all, when you enter into a busy market with lower inventory, there will be much less competition for the fixer upper. Many other prospective home buyers may see the property as an "ugly duckling", not realizing the full potential of the "diamond in the rough". You have a higher likelihood of your offer being accepted on the home and having the opportunity to make it into everything you imagined it could be. Renovation loans
allow the buyer to customize the home and make it the way they want right from the start. This type of lending also allows for instant equity the very same day you purchase the home.

What are some common misconceptions homebuyers have about funding a home purchase through renovation lending?

David Lewis: Because of the misconceptions that exist about renovation lending, I have been on a mission to educate the public on this financing option. Many mortgage professionals in today's industry are aware of the product, but not well versed enough to present it as a benefit to potential home buyers. Often times, a loan officer will try to avoid this type of deal altogether because they feel it will be more work to close on their end. Real estate agents also tend to use the avoidance tactic because they are under the false impression that renovation loans take longer and are more difficult to close. These misconceptions prevent loan officers from acting in the best interests of their clients. In most cases, the deal ends up taking longer or falling through because the loan officer does not have the knowledge to lead the client successfully though each milestone of a renovation loan. This is where I take pride in many years of experience helping home buyers to purchase and renovate in one smooth process.

What perceived obstacles arise during the renovation loan process and how can these be avoided?

David Lewis: One obstacle that I come across on both the professional and consumer side is a feeling of being prohibited by cost. There is a misconception that a renovation loan will be much more expensive than a typical loan. While there are more fees involved which are associated with the construction portion, these are able to be financed into the loan. It is not more expensive to close a renovation loan. The renovation loans that I work with exclusively are agency loans. Identical to 95% of the mortgages done in this country, they are Fannie Mae or FHA based. They are exactly the same in nature as typical loans, simply with an added provision for renovation.

What pitfalls and common mistakes do people encounter during the renovation loan process and how can these be avoided?

David Lewis: One of the biggest pitfalls that people encounter is not realizing they need renovation financing until after they've entered into a contract. Most people feel like they can buy a fixer upper with a regular loan. And while that can be true, there are often definite health and safety issues associated with these types of properties. And it's usually not until well after they've signed a purchase agreement that they realize a renovation loan would have been in their best interest.

Secondly, I come across many clients who want to do the work themselves or to have a blood relative be their contractor. Choosing a qualified contractor is paramount in the renovation process. I coach and

consult my clients on selecting the proper professionals to perform the renovation. It is crucial to have work completed in a timely manner. After all, nobody wants to live in a construction zone after
purchasing their first home. Finding a contractor that can complete the work in an acceptable time frame, but also with care and precision, should always be the end goal.

Can you share an example of how you have helped your clients successfully navigate renovation lending?

David Lewis: Throughout my career, I have had many positive experiences helping clients navigate renovation lending. Two examples stick with me. The first one was a young couple in New York and their goal and desire was to live in the neighborhood where the wife grew up. Though they were doing well for themselves making great salaries, the neighborhood was cost prohibitive simply due to location and the price point of the homes in that particular area. They stumbled upon a bank owned property going for much, much less than the market value for the neighborhood. It was serendipity that they found me because even though the house was affordable, they couldn't close on it with a regular mortgage because of the condition it was in. Being bank owned and abandoned, it lacked many of the utilities needed for a functioning home. After meeting with me, they entered into a renovation loan. They were unaware of this option and were so excited to find out they could borrow money not only to complete the repairs, but that these desired renovations could be rolled into one affordable loan. The purchase price of the home was around $300,000. The couple decided on $300,000 worth of renovation for a total renovation loan of $600,000. Our appraisal, based on all the anticipated work, was 1.2 million. At the end of the day, the couple owed the bank $600,000 which is not a small loan by any means. However, their equity position in this case doubled. Through the power of renovation lending, this couple was able to move into their dream neighborhood which once seemed out of reach. In addition, they were able to cost effectively borrow the funds to turn the house into everything they wanted it to be, all within their particular budget.

The second example involves a newly married couple pregnant with their first child. This couple had very specific needs regarding location. Due to family planning and careers, they desired a home close to in-laws, their places of employment, shopping, etc. As they looked at homes, they began to see the challenges of searching within a specific location range. Though they had no problem finding homes in the area of choice, the houses themselves were coming up short of their expectations. One of these homes was a two-bedroom, one bath, smaller Cape Cod. They were in love with the location but struggled to see how their family could grow and thrive in a home this size. After some research, they found me and again, through the power of renovation lending, we were able to make this home into everything they needed it to be. We found a contractor and turned the home into a three-bedroom, two bath with many updates including HVAC system, new roofing, siding, and windows. In the end, they had about $22,000 in equity after doing a hundred-thousand-dollar renovation on top of the purchase price. They were easily able to afford the renovation money into their 30-year mortgage with a fixed rate.

Any advice for first time home buyers looking for fixer uppers and interested in renovation lending? How should they begin the process?

David Lewis: One of the things that I teach my clients is to go to any real estate website, which there are no shortage of these days. So, let's just use Zillow for an example. They can go into Zillow and narrow down their state, city, town, neighborhood, or whatever criteria they desire. I then advise to go into the advanced search area of Zillow and type a keyword like "TLC". Other keywords could include "handyman special", "investor only", or "cash only". I prefer the term "TLC" because it is a nice way to reveal the homes that need work and the listings will come right up.

More importantly, I guide my clients further by telling them that realtors don't really know how to handle these listings and are unaware that regular financing will not allow them to close. They may have had experience with substandard properties that have made it almost all the way through the mortgage transaction and failed to close because of the condition of the property. This is why it is so important for the buyer to come in loaded with knowledge of renovation lending and why it is my mission to provide this knowledge. I encourage first time home buyers to search their local market area for an expert in renovation lending to successfully guide them through the process.

Often times, clients end up finding homes that are in move in condition. They may think a renovation loan is unnecessary. However, in most areas of the country, the average age of a home is in excess of 35 years. Which can only mean one thing ...the home is going to need work. Armed with renovation loan knowledge, even if the kitchen was outdated, there was no garage, the ceiling was cracking, the siding needed to be replaced, etc. you are able to make an educated offer on the home and borrow effectively the money you need to fix it or create your vision. If I can get to a client in the preapproval stage and educate them, they are prepared with all the information necessary to make a better buying decision for their family.

What inspired you to get into renovation lending?

David Lewis: When I first got into the business, I was allowed to answer inbound calls. This was 25 years ago when landlines were the lifeblood of any business. Being on the phone allowed for great opportunities and sure enough, the first call I took was a gentleman looking to purchase a home that was in disrepair. He wasn't sure what he needed to do or where to turn for help with the loan. It just so happened that the company I was working for at the time was the national leader in renovation loans. I wasn't even too familiar with them yet, but I knew they existed. So, I said, "Hey, why don't you try out one of these?" I went out to his house, met him and took his loan application. When I got back to the office, I obviously needed a lot of help. We completed the renovation loan process and the client was over the moon. He wasn't only happy that he got the house, but appreciative that I solved a problem for him that he could not solve on his own. I made the renovations of the home that were necessary and desired very cost effective for him and his family. I discovered right away that there was power in that. From

there I trained with some of the people in my company that were very well adept with this kind of financing and did renovation loans almost exclusively. The moment that really solidified it for me was
when I went to train with a mentor and she had a line of about 10 people waiting to start the application process. Renovation lending was her specialty and back then there were very few loan officers who knew how to handle these types of loans. From that moment, I was hooked. I was

really helping people... getting them a mortgage, working hard to save them money on their closing costs, negotiating to get them the best rate available at the time and having them close on time left me with a very satisfying feeling. In one easy loan, I was able to help people build instant equity and make repairs on the home in a very cost-effective way. I was fortunate enough to have my first loan experience be a renovation loan which instilled the passion that still drives me today.

Can you share a lesson learned early on that still impacts how you do business today?

David Lewis: First of all, honest and open communication with clients is so important. I pride myself on keeping an open mind to the fact that no matter how long I am in this business, I will never know everything. I have realized it is okay to say "I don't know the answer to that. There are probably a couple different correct answers but let me do the research and find the one that is the best fit for you." As long as there is some good, educated follow up, it is okay to not have all the answers immediately.

The second lesson I learned early on when it comes to renovation loans is managing expectations up front with everyone. Be firm in making your clients truly understand the process. In this industry, many people are pushovers with clients and realtor partners because they feel that if they push back a little, they will never get the referral. At the end of the day, if you stand your ground based on knowledge, you gain more respect, and ultimately, more referrals.

What is the most important thing home buyers should consider when evaluating a renovation lender?

David Lewis: You definitely want a lender with experience. Behind every loan officer are operation people...processing, underwriting, closing. Each of these individuals should be well aware of the process and have experience with these particular loans.

Secondly, do not try to over improve for your area. For example, if the home you are renovating is in a $300,000 neighborhood, do not try to renovate into a $450,000 house. Know the value of the homes in the area and renovate to the top of the value...not over the top.

How can someone find out more about David Lewis and how you can help?

David Lewis: I offer every potential client an absolutely free, no pressure, no obligation, no money consultation for renovation lending and how it works. The educator side of me loves helping people feel informed and prepared. The best way to contact me is my direct line: 978-423-2254.

DAVID LEWIS

Renovation Lending Expert

David has spent the past 25 years working in the Mortgage Industry. His superpowers come from helping literally thousands of families successfully navigate through the renovation loan process. David's years of experience and unsurpassed knowledge of Renovation Lending have given him the unique ability to elevate the Renovation Lending customer experience well above industry standards.

Born and raised in Massachusetts, David Lewis now resides in the state of Connecticut with his beautiful wife, Gina, and their awesome Blue French Bulldog, Sir Maxximus Blu.

EMAIL: djlmarketing@gmail.com

LINKEDIN: https://www.linkedin.com/in/djlmarketing/

FACEBOOK:

https://www.facebook.com/RenovationMortgageExpert/

PHONE: (978) 423-2254

JASON DUPONT

Knowledge is Power on the Path to Homeownership

Conversation with Jason Dupont

Tell us about AZ Home Loans and the types of clients that you can help.:

Jason Dupont: AZ Home Loans started out as Affinity Mortgage. I began working for them a little over two years ago and shortly thereafter it became AZ Home Loans. The philosophy behind the company is to offer no lender fees without compromising customer service. In fact, we strive to offer superior service as well as the lowest costs for our clients. As part of our no lender fee business model, we make less per loan and strive for customer referrals to achieve a high-volume approach. Think of AZ Home Loans like the Costco of mortgages...more volume married to amazing customer service. About 90% of the clients we serve are purchase transactions. Although we focus on purchases, we also do refinancing. Our bread and butter are just normal, Conventional, VA, FHA, and USDA loans. However, we pride ourselves on being able to handle more complicated loans as well. We can conquer unique situations like self-employed clients and alternate credit/income routes to help as many people as possible achieve their home buying dreams. So, the clients we serve are anyone who is looking for excellent customer service and the best bang for their buck.

What are the advantages or benefits of working with you and AZ Home Loans over other options potential homebuyers may have?

Jason Dupont: Since AZ Home Loans is a broker, we have very low overhead. That translates to advantages for our clients; there are no lending fees whatsoever: no underwriting, no processing, no credit report, and no application fees. Additionally, our company has employees that are credit specialists. If someone is in need of credit repair, we can address that issue right in house. Not every client is ready to purchase when they come to us. Because our company is relationship driven, we do not turn people away. We always work with each and every individual to get them on a timeline to complete the steps necessary to get them into a home as quickly as possible. In addition, we have in house underwriting. We go the extra mile by having our underwriters go through all the client documents and issuing a preapproval. This saves the client a lot of time and effort when the contract comes in. It also allows the offer to be stronger, with an average 21 day close. Although it is not quite as strong as a cash offer, having the potential buyer pre-approved is the next best thing.

What do you feel are the biggest myths or misconceptions out there when it comes to funding a property?

Jason Dupont: The biggest myths revolve around credit scores and how much is needed to put down on a home. A lot of people think that you need to put down 20% down. They believe that a home purchase is not in the cards until they have saved that amount of money. In reality, there are quite a few amazing programs out there involving as little as 3% down payments.

Another myth involves people thinking they should find their dream home first, then meet with a loan officer. I understand why the industry runs backwards in this way...people get emotionally attached to a home, not a loan. However, if a realtor is showing you homes before you qualify, the entire process can be very disheartening. If you meet with a mortgage professional first, you will know what you qualify for and whether you are shopping in the right price range. And if a higher price range is what you are after, you have a loan officer to guide you through the steps to get there. Often, there is a house on the market with several competing offers. Instead of having to rush through the entire process from scratch and potentially missing your chance on putting in an offer, you will have your prequalification ready to go by meeting with a loan officer first.

One of our seasoned loan officers can help dispel all of the myths about what it takes to get into a home. We are here to counsel and educate. Unlike many other mortgage companies, we are not trained to be salespeople. With our no fee approach, we don't need to sell because we already have amazing rates. This allows our entire approach to be education based and focused on the unique needs of each client.

What are some little-known pitfalls or common mistakes you see homebuyers make on the road to getting a mortgage?

Jason Dupont: We work with a lot of different realtors and a lot of different clients. Our reviews are amazing and that's one thing we take pride in. As mentioned previously, one of the common mistakes I see is clients looking for a home before their prequalification. In addition, we see many clients that may have been working with another lender where the transaction fell apart and they come to us trying to pick up the pieces. For example, some clients make large purchases during the transaction. When you are in the thick of the home buying process, you can't just go buy a car right before you close. You don't want to make any purchases during that transaction because the loan is being underwritten to your current credit picture. You certainly do not want to change that picture, especially in an extreme manner. You are given your rate based on a risk-based analysis and loan type. The three main pieces considered in the loan process are the equity or down payment, the credit and the income. Once you learn about credit and how it affects you, we have ways to get that credit where it needs to be.

What inspired you to get into the mortgage industry?

Jason Dupont: When I was in my early twenties, I got a job at a call center in a bank. It was my responsibility to open new accounts. From this experience, I learned that banks are primarily relationship based. I didn't obtain just one piece of a client's financial history. I obtained it all so that I could offer a wide variety of services including credit cards, debit cards, savings accounts, investment services, personal loans, business loans, and home equity loans. From that experience, I developed a passion for the lending side.

Of all the products I was able to offer, I always gravitated to mortgage lending.

In addition, I was inspired to help people in an industry that I felt was a little bit "broken". So many people wanted to get into homes but were uneducated about the process. In the late nineties people were being taken advantage of, especially the elderly, due to this lack of knowledge. It became my own personal mission to learn the ins and outs of the industry so that I could pass this information on to my clients and help them achieve homeownership with confidence.

Do you have an example of one of the most interesting or challenging mortgages that you were able to get approved?

Jason Dupont: A client came to me post mortgage meltdown. He had a decent credit score and a small amount of money saved up for the down payment. He was moving to Arizona from California. The borrower disclosed he had a short sale property which occurred approximately ten years prior. This would have no effect on the current loan. Near the closing of the loan, our research revealed that the short sale was actually a foreclosure. Since we were doing a conventional loan with 5% down, one of the guidelines is that you cannot have a foreclosure in the last seven years. I sat the borrower down and had a conversation about what happened. During the mortgage crash, he wanted to give the house back and was under the impression that he was going through a short sale. He moved into an apartment. Due to the madness of everything going on during the crash, the lender took three full years to foreclose on the original property. So, he moved out, stopped paying on it, and thought he was going through a short sale process, due to that lack of knowledge that I referred to earlier. When the borrower told me it had been 10 years, he was truly being honest based off memory. But it ended up being under seven years because of the time it took for the lender to foreclose. We were left scrambling. He did not have 20% to put down, we were limited as to other available products.

I had to think outside of the box and find a way to get this client into a home. The purchase price was around $380,000 and the FHA loan limit was $314,000 and change. So, we decided to go FHA and take out a second mortgage with a concurrent close, to make up for the difference. His credit score was high enough to make this possible. The institution that we used did not care about the foreclosure within the last seven years and my client qualified. He was extremely happy, and our realtor partner was very happy. No one had ever seen anything like that done before. I worked diligently to find a way to do it and help the client reach their ultimate goal of a funded loan.

Can you share a lesson that you learned early on that still impacts how you do business today?

Jason Dupont: When I started in this industry, we filled out everything by hand. We had a packet for every loan, and we would fill it out, calculate a good faith estimate, rates and annual percentage rates. We would typically do this during a face to face meeting with clients in their homes. One evening, back in 1997, I was calling some of my mortgage leads from home. I had an absolutely wonderful conversation with a lady, took her application via phone and planned to meet her at her home the next evening to collect documents. An important aspect of this story is that earlier in that same day, I had lost a loan. The borrower lied to me and provided misinformation which resulted in the loan being denied very close to funding. I was very frustrated by this and learned a valuable lesson when I allowed that frustration to carry over into my current conversation with the new client. At the end of the call, she asked "Jason, what do you think my chances are?" I responded, "Pretty good, as long as you are not lying to me." It was probably the worst thing I could have ever said, and it instantly killed the relationship. I'm really big on building relationships, being transparent, and being honest. People find my transparency and honesty refreshing because we live in a world where everyone is trying to sell everyone all the time. I will never forget that experience because it taught me that you have to be able to let things go and not dump any baggage that you are carrying onto others. It was not only a lesson in the mortgage industry, but a significant life lesson as well.

What are the most important things homebuyers should consider when evaluating a potential mortgage broker?

Jason Dupont: It is important to choose someone that you connect with. Find someone that you can respect and trust. A home purchase involves a long process of trust building and you need someone who will spend the time and energy to nurture that relationship. It isn't like a car sale where you meet your sales guy and take the car home that night. There is time involved in the prequalification process and shopping for a home. You will have many questions and will need someone to answer those questions and hold your hand through the entire process, whether it be your first or your fifth home.

How can someone find out more about you, AZ Home Loans, and how you can help?

Jason Dupont: You can contact me via cell at 480-201-7225. I am on Facebook under Jason Dupont. And, anyone who is an avid cyclist like me, can find me on Strava. I am always available for questions. Even if you are working with another lender and wonder if you are getting a good deal, shoot me a text message or reach out on Facebook and I can offer my guidance. I look forward to sharing the knowledge that can lead you to the home of your dreams.

JASON DUPONT

General Manager

AZ Home Loans

Jason is an avid cyclist, a committed husband, and a dedicated father of five children. He originated his first mortgage loan in 1997. His team works to ensure each individual they serve knows their best interest is at heart. Jason prides himself in being hard working, reliable, and ensuring clients are coached throughout the home loan process. His goal is to create a positive experience for everyone he assists. He is very knowledgeable, a problem solver, and detail oriented. Jason recognizes that good communication with clients is a must – office, phone, text or email, he's available for you. He looks forward to the opportunity to show you what he can do!

His personal motto is: If you are on the right path, it will always be uphill...

WEBSITE: AZHomeLoans.com

EMAIL: jdupont@azhomeloans.com

FACEBOOK:

https://www.facebook.com/stumblehere.classifieds

INSTAGRAM:

https://www.instagram.com/home.loan.cyclist/

STRAVA:

https://www.strava.com/athletes/jason_dupont

PHONE: (480) 201-7225

AMANDA MADSEN

Mortgages for the Self-Employed...Approved!

Conversation with Amanda Madsen

Tell us about yourself and how you are helping your clients:

Amanda Madsen: I am a mortgage loan originator and I help all buyers. One of my specialties that I devote a lot of time and attention to is helping self-employed borrowers. After the crash of our mortgage and real estate industry, it became very challenging for self-employed borrowers to get into a home. Being a self-employed person almost all of my adult life, I found this to be unfair. Encouragingly, now we are seeing the guidelines start to change and lighten up. But when I first got started in the industry, I realized that it was an injustice because we work really hard as self-employed people or entrepreneurs and are not given the opportunity to understand what the mortgage process looks like or how to get into a home. I took it upon myself to dive in and really give people that chance.

Can you tell us the number one challenge self-employed buyers face when it comes to getting a mortgage?

Amanda Madsen: Self-employed borrowers know how much they really make and when they do their taxes, they are trying to avoid paying a lot. Because of the structuring of these particular taxes, there are components in the process that even CPAs do not fully understand. Many times, I have a client come to me and tell me that they make x amount of dollars and it adds up to a nice, healthy living. But when you take a look at their taxes and the amount we can actually lend on; it is a very different number. I really take the time to help my clients understand why this happens and what steps we can take to get them into a home. Often, my borrowers have had to wait to get into a home. In this case, we strategize and collaborate with the CPA who can help put some of the write offs and expenses into the correct category which would be more beneficial to the borrowers. As a team, we determine what can give the client more buying power moving forward.

Is there a solution for self-employed borrowers who may have been doing their taxes incorrectly?

Amanda Madsen: There is a way to remedy this situation early in the process. Ideally, I like to speak with self-employed borrowers immediately about their taxes and if possible, before tax season comes. If the client comes to me already having done them incorrectly, perhaps took a whole lot of deductions, for example, they have an option to do an amendment to their taxes. I leave that up to the client and the CPA to have the conversation about what would be in the client's best financial interest. It truly is up to the borrower and dependent on their comfortability with amendments being suggested.

One client who I helped navigate the tax process and continue to help to this day actually nicknamed me "the mortgage wizard." He was self-employed and desperately wanting to get into a home. After being denied a mortgage two times previously, he was rather skeptical about working with me. When we did get him the home of his dreams, he was elated and couldn't believe it was really happening for him. From that point, he expressed his interest in buying more properties and so every year, we sit down together and strategize about doing his taxes in order to give him the purchasing power that he had been in search of for so long.

What are the biggest myths out there when it comes to getting a mortgage for a self-employed individual or business owner?

Amanda Madsen: The media often spreads the myth that buying a home isn't a good idea. In my professional experience, I have witnessed my self-employed borrowers gain so much wealth and growth from becoming homeowners. It is really important to understand how much value there is behind owning a home and how it benefits your financial future in a variety of ways. A mortgage originator who specializes in helping self-employed people reach this goal and who is skilled at developing a game plan to get over the hurdles of the mortgage process is a key element in busting myths and making homeownership attainable.

Are there common fears that self-employed clients have about obtaining a mortgage?

Amanda Madsen: Self-employed people often have a concern about where the money is going to come from. How can I know how my business will do year to year based on the economy? Are the rates going to be good? Do I have enough money for a down payment? Many people are still under the misconception that you need 20% down in order to get into a home. This is simply not true, and borrowers should not allow this to discourage them.

Often, self-employed borrowers fear that they do not make enough money, their credit scores aren't great, or that their debt to income ratios might be off due to debt associated with the business. There are avenues that you can go down to remedy this situation. For example, if you have a lot of business debt on your personal credit card, it can affect your debt to income ratio negatively. I encourage clients to make business payments out of an exclusive business account. These can then be reduced and excluded from your debt income, thus giving you significantly more buying power. Since self-employed borrowers are challenged with many more fears and uncertainties, meeting with a skilled loan officer is a great first step in gaining clarity.

What is a common mistake that self-employed buyers make that may complicate the mortgage process?

Amanda Madsen: The most mistakes are commonly made on taxes. We have to be very conscious of this when reviewing the tax structure. There are many deductions that people are unaware of. One of the things that often hinders my clients from getting their preferred home or getting into a home altogether is placing deductions in the wrong area. One of those areas is depreciation. Depreciation is a really great thing because you're purchasing something for your business to grow your business. And you can also use that as qualifying income, but it has to be in the depreciation section.

Mileage is another important factor. I have noticed that many CPAs don't always give their self-employed borrowers mileage deductions. We actually have a formula that we can use for mileage that can give additional income to the home buyer. I have seen mileage save deals or simply help clients get over a debt to income ratio hump.

There are times when I get pushback from CPAs during conversations about tax structure. It can be challenging for them to step outside of their traditional ways of doing things. But it is my job to strive for collaboration and help my borrowers achieve their homeownership goals.

Can you share an example of how you helped a client through a challenging situation to achieve their homeownership dreams?

Amanda Madsen: A story that stands out in my mind involves a young man whose father was an entrepreneur and an income property owner. So, he had watched his dad own multiple properties and saw the success and financial growth that came with it. He was self-employed, driven, and very much wanted to become a homeowner, even immediately after the crash of our real estate industry. It had been very challenging for him and it took him awhile to gain my trust after he was declined two times and lost earnest money twice previously. After developing a solid foundation of trust, I helped him acquire his first home. It was a duplex and he only had to put 3.5% down because it was his primary residence and with the FHA loan, his mortgage was instantly offset with the additional home (duplex). This gave him a leg up creating more cash flow and ability to do more with his money while building his business.

He later got married and the couple decided they would like to search for another home. Him and I stayed in contact and we structured a strategy for him to continue to create more growth in his business with his taxes. And at the time, he didn't realize that every time we spoke I was setting him up for success in our conversation. And when it came time to buy a second home, we used the income from his previous duplexes to help give him purchasing power toward the new home. Since then, he has purchased several other homes and even has a cabin that he rents out and makes money, hand over fist. It is astonishing how much he is making on that cabin in a resort town in addition to some other homes.

Not only did I help him create more cash flow in his current business, but I helped him to create another business of income properties. We have strategized together for the past six years and are continually coming up with ways to achieve his next goal. I use him as an example often because he went from a young kid with almost nothing, to an adult who has great cash flow and owns multiple properties, all before the age of 30. It has been an honor to be part of his journey to success and growth.

What inspired you to get into the mortgage business and eventually to your specialization of working with self-employed buyers?

Amanda Madsen: I was a single mom at age 19, starting my journey as a hairstylist, and I was experiencing firsthand the struggles of being a self-employed person. I had been a hairstylist for about 18 years when I realized I was never going to retire in this profession. My body was getting sore and tired and I was ready for a change. One of my clients at the time was a loan officer and there was something about it that struck me when we would talk about her job. In addition, I had never been a homeowner and thought it was an unattainable goal. It seemed like a great career move for me to go into a field where I could learn all about how to make my own dream of homeownership come true.

After working in the service industry for so long, creating rapport, listening to clients and developing relationships, I found that these skills lend very well to the mortgage industry. I listen intently to my borrowers needs and have very clear, clean dialogue on how we're going to achieve their goals. And because I had many of the same fears when I was self-employed, I am able to relate well to my clients. It really brings everything full circle for me as I am helping them achieve the same goals I had for myself.

Can you share a lesson you learned early on that still impacts how you do business today?

Amanda Madsen: Throughout my professional journey, I have worked with and helped people of all walks of life: wealthy, poor, young, old, confident and broken. No matter who they were or what they did, I have always enjoyed hearing their life stories, goals, and dreams. I have learned that everyone deserves the same chances and opportunities at achieving their goals. I have also learned that compassion and understanding go a very long way. Statistics show that home ownership is one of the best ways to create wealth for people, and I feel very fortunate to be able to guide clients through that process.

Is there anything that you feel potential home buyers should consider when evaluating and choosing a loan officer?

Amanda Madsen: It is very important to find someone who is willing to take the time to sit down and have a conversation with you, help you understand the process, and reveal the benefits that you have working in your favor already that you weren't aware of. Knowledge really becomes your power when it comes to homeownership. Find a loan officer who will not only share knowledge but share in the desire to achieve your homeownership goals.

How can someone find out more about you and how you can help?

Amanda Madsen: The best way to reach me is via email at amanda.madsen@snmc.com. My direct website is Snmc.com/amandamadsen. Here you can find all my information, applications, testimonials, etc. I look forward to helping you realize your dreams of homeownership are not out of reach!

AMANDA MADSEN

Mortgage Specialist, NMLS# 220721

Security National Mortgage Company
NMLS#3116

Amanda is a professional loan originator who focuses on solutions and satisfaction for each of her client's unique situations. Whether you are looking for a new loan with great terms, or finding a better refinance solution, she will individually consult with you to ensure that you are offered a full line of loan product solutions that best match your unique needs and financial situation. Amanda believes in effective communication with each client throughout the entire business transaction and strives to build a relationship that continues long after the loan is closed. She is committed to earning your business and respect every time you choose to do business with her and refer others to engage her services.

Amanda looks forward to better understanding your personal loan needs and finding the best solution. She will work with you to help accomplish your financial goals. Clear communication is critical in this process so her team will keep you updated every step of the way. This communication will help build a relationship that will last, and her goal is to help you be satisfied with each transaction. Her clients are the best resource for new business and her service is a key to success in helping her earn your referrals. Amanda looks forward to the opportunity to earn your business and is confident you will be very happy!

WEBSITE: Snmc.com/amandamadsen and

Yourmortgagewizard.com

EMAIL: Amanda.madsen@snmc.com

FACEBOOK:

https://www.facebook.com/YourMortgageWizard/

LINKEDIN: https://www.linkedin.com/in/amanda-madsen/

OFFICE: 801-508-6300

CELL: 801-577-5137

FAX: 801-508-3601

MANNY YAQUIAN

The Benefits of Homeownership Within Your Reach

Conversation with Manny Yaquian

Tell us about yourself and how you are helping your clients:

Manny Yaquian: My first name is Manrique, but for the sake of clients being able to pronounce my name, I go by Manny. I have been in the mortgage industry for over 10 years as a mortgage originator and currently am with Caliber Home Loans Inc., which is the second largest mortgage lender by volume in the country (Scotsman Guide, 2019). My niche is in the San Antonio, Texas market. I have a team that supports follow-up with the clients, meets their needs, and provides the warm fuzzy feeling that these clients desire during the home buying process. We support a very hands on approach, giving this huge corporate machine of a company a very accessible, local presence.

Both myself and my company pride ourselves on using industry leading technology but also providing elite service. A new, exciting venture that we are offering to our clients is changing the way the home buying process plays out. The traditional home buying process would involve the client going to a realtor, finding the home they wanted, and then going through the mortgage process. Now, we are taking the initiative by going directly to employers, fortune 500 companies, and small businesses to provide closing cost discounts to employees that get their home financing through us. In this way, the financing can be taken care of before the client even goes to look for a home. Employers are jumping on board and ironically enough, a recent study just revealed that employees that own their own home are more than 70% more likely to stay with their employer than employees who do not own a home. So, it becomes in the best interest of the employer to help their employees in the home buying process and we love being able to cultivate this relationship.

What is the number one challenge that potential homebuyers encounter during the mortgage process? What is their biggest concern?

Manny Yaquian: Dealing with the financing process of a mortgage is a transaction that most individuals will only do twice in their lifetime. So, preparing themselves for that process is a common concern. I compare it to when I had my firstborn... I read so many books on how to be a dad and I was still a deer in the headlights when my daughter came into the world. I tell all my clients not to stress about preparing 100% for the process. They just need to allow themselves to be guided correctly and establish a comfortability and trust with their mortgage loan originator. We strive to develop that personal relationship because honestly, we are obtaining someone's entire financial background in a short period. This entails financial history, credit history, deposit history, etc. Getting to that trust level is not an easy process and this ends up being a concern for many clients initially. We want our clients to achieve a high level of comfort, first and foremost.

What are the advantages for businesses that choose to work with you and Caliber Home Loans to set up employee mortgage plans?

Manny Yaquian: In addition to the statistic mentioned above regarding the loyalty of homeowners to a business, there are other advantages. First, they will be working with a reputable mortgage lender that services the entire country. They automatically have someone they can trust and who can handle the mortgage process for their employees in a smooth and knowledgeable fashion. We can also offer discounts towards the actual cost of the mortgage process and on closing costs. In addition, we can set up workshops and home buying seminars for the employees at their place of business. They are receiving hands on exposure and even a referral network of originators nationwide. Many larger businesses enjoy the benefit of being able to deal with Caliber Home Loans no matter what part of the country the branch is located. Employee mortgage plans end up being a win-win situation for both employer and employee.

What do you feel are the biggest myths out there when it comes to funding a home purchase?

Manny Yaquian: One of the most common myths that I come across is primarily stemming from the newer generation that I do business with. They all tend to think that putting 20% down is a necessary requirement. That is simply not correct. The truth of the matter is that there are programs with down payment requirements, the smallest being zero, for first time home buyers and the added benefit of putting money down. Sure, it can provide better control of your budget if you can put 20% down, but it is certainly not a must.

Other myths that exist revolve around employment. Clients are often concerned that if they had multiple employers in the past two years, they will not qualify for a mortgage. Similarly, people who can further themselves via promotion or changing job fields will not experience negative side effects in the mortgage process. It is important that these changes are fully disclosed to your mortgage loan originator, however it shouldn't cause fear for being denied a loan.

The most important advice I give when applying for a loan is "be transparent". The more transparent you can be will help us get you into your dream home in a timely fashion.

What perceived obstacles exist for people trying to obtain a home loan?

Manny Yaquian: Student loan debt is a very common perceived obstacle that I encounter. I see many schoolteachers furthering their careers and stacking up six figure student loan amounts along the way. People often feel that this will affect their ability to get approved for a mortgage. The amount of student loan debt doesn't always impact obtaining a home loan. There are many programs in existence that help individuals with student loan debt on their journey to homeownership.

Another obstacle is what I like to refer to as "purchasing power". What I mean by this term is what a person feels they can afford compared to what they can qualify for. For example, let's look at a client who comes to me and says they can afford $2,000 monthly payments. They base this off what their rent and bills are currently and feel comfortable knowing they can accomplish this payment. However, after officially going through the mortgage process, they may qualify for $1,500 a month. That gap is the purchasing power and often seen as an obstacle for most people. To overcome that obstacle, we help them fill in the gap. Maybe there are things we can update, a down payment that can be made, or a loan program that can offer better interest rates to increase purchasing power. In any case, preparation and getting your trusted mortgage advisor involved early in the process is very beneficial in avoiding any perceived obstacles altogether.

What are some pitfalls or little-known mistakes that homebuyers make on the road to getting a mortgage?

Manny Yaquian: Can I answer this one by saying "Not using me as their mortgage guy?" In all seriousness, home buyers need to do their research to find someone that is dedicated to the mortgage and will follow through with the process. Make sure that the people you do business with are actively presenting themselves on social media, have great reviews, and good exposure within the company they work for. The biggest purchase of your life deserves the dedication of time and energy to find a mortgage professional that you can trust and feel confident about.

What do you offer uniquely for your clients as opposed to competitors or online mortgage companies?

Manny Yaquian: One thing that is unique about Caliber Home Loans is that we service many loans we originate and close. Our clients have the peace of mind that their loan will be taken care of throughout the application process, at the end of closing, and over the lifetime of the client making their payments. This gives us a great advantage in building relationships with our clients that continue over the course of the entire loan.

Another benefit of working with our company is the option of portfolio loans. These loans offer progressive, innovative solutions to common lending barriers. For example, we help people with issues such as bankruptcy, short sales, foreclosures etc. We consider these areas a bit deeper to help clients who may feel discouraged and out of options.

What inspired you to start a career in the mortgage industry?

Manny Yaquian: To be honest, I couldn't even spell mortgage as I graduated with a degree in international business and a minor in finance. I studied abroad and never even gave any thought to mortgages. In 2007, a good friend of mine who was working for a large bank contacted me and asked if I would like to work in the mortgage industry with him. So, the job kind of fell in my lap but I have learned to appreciate it, the relationships I have built, and the many families I have could help. And even though I landed a job in the industry by pure luck, I wouldn't change it for the world. The rewarding feeling I get from helping families achieve their dreams of homeownership is one that has kept me in the industry and will continue to do so for years to come.

Can you share a lesson you learned early on that still impacts how you do business today?

Manny Yaquian: Proactive and not reactive is a strategy that I have when it comes to coaching within my own team. When it comes to the expectations of clients or referral partners, proactive communication has helped me gain a better network of repeat business. My team can grow more business by educating our clients, keeping them informed, and managing their expectations. We have many platforms to accomplish this including seminars at local levels and online websites that can be accessed through portals on phones and apps. Keeping clients educated through a variety of channels is something I pride myself on and will continue to do.

What are the most important questions homebuyers should ask themselves as they consider getting a mortgage?

Manny Yaquian: The first question should be "Why haven't I thought about this sooner?" A Vice President that I used to work with would always say "Manny...the best time to buy a home was always yesterday." Though I didn't quite understand what he meant at the time, that statement has so much truth to it. When you think of things such as market volatility and what you are paying for rent monthly that goes into an asset you have no ownership or equity built into, homeownership is a great decision! Once people get past the fears and misconceptions and enter the mortgage process with us, they realize that the path to owning a home is quite smooth. I encourage people to take that step, regardless of what stage of life you are in. Add another pillar to your financial strength by protecting your assets and taking pride in something you can pass down from generation to generation ...a home!

What is the most important thing home buyers should consider when evaluating a lender?

Manny Yaquian: They should certainly consider the years of experience that the loan originator has. Make sure that the loan originator maintains public transparency and has multiple, credible reviews. Also, you can always call an originator and conduct an interview with them asking about specific experience in the industry and to better determine if they will be able to help you meet your homeownership goals. It is always positive to see large mortgage companies like Caliber Home Loans who can take on new ventures and constantly on a mission to help more families.

How can someone find out more about you, Caliber Home Loans, and how you can help?

Manny Yaquian: Looking me up online is the most efficient way to start. Potential clients can search Google, Facebook, Yelp, or Zillow under the Manny Yaquian Team to find out more about what we do with Caliber Home Loans. From there, you can feel free to call or shoot me a quick text...I am always going to pick up my phone. I look forward to guiding you on the path to home ownership.

MANNY YAQUIAN

Sales Manager / Mortgage Loan Originator, NMLS 511147

Caliber Home Loans Inc.

With 10 years of experience in the Texas mortgage industry, Manny has the knowledge and dedication required to provide you with the ideal home financing.

Caliber's competitive rates, combined with state-of-the-art technology, enable him to offer you one or more customized loan options. You can rely on Manny to assist you with home financing that provides lasting affordability and value, and to work hard to address your needs while closing your loan as quickly as possible. Both first time buyers and seasoned mortgage applicants rely on his integrity and skills for a tailored mortgage transaction. He considers it an honor to assist our veterans and active duty military personnel, whether you've just received a PCS or planning a local move.

Manny also believes that the key to service is to combine old-fashioned customer service with high-tech efficiency. And since Caliber is a dedicated lender, he can offer you a wider selection of loan products than many banking institutions.

Before entering the home loan industry, Manny graduated from St. Mary's University with a BBA degree before earning his MBA from University of Phoenix. His professional affiliations include membership in Lambda Chi Alpha. When not assisting customers with their home loans, Manny enjoys time with family and friends at church functions and barbeques.

He thanks you in advance for the opportunity to assist you with one of life's most important financial transactions.

WEBSITE: www.caliberhomeloans.com/myaquian

EMAIL: Manrique.yaquian@caliberhomeloans.com

FACEBOOK: Manny Yaquian Team

PHONE: (210) 885-3108

FAX: (855) 734-6522

Disclaimers:

This is an advertisement from Caliber Home Loans, Inc. Caliber Home Loans, Inc. and any mentioned companies are not affiliated.

Scotsman Guide's Top Mortgage Lenders 2019 rankings available at [www.scotsmanguide.com/Rankings/Top-Lenders-2018/Results/Top-Overall-Volume/].

Discounts apply to direct originations made by Caliber Home Loans, Inc. and are not available on loans obtained through external mortgage brokers. Discounts apply to first mortgage purchase or refinance transactions. Not available on home equity loans or lines of credit

Caliber Home Loans, Inc., 1525 S. Beltline Rd Coppell, TX 75019 NMLS ID #15622 (www.nmlsconsumeraccess.org). 1-800-401-6587. Copyright © 2019. All Rights Reserved. [Equal Housing Lender.] This is not an offer to enter into an agreement. Not all customers will qualify. Information, rates, and programs are subject to change without prior notice. All products are subject to credit and property approval. Not all products are available in all states or for all dollar amounts. Other restrictions and limitations apply.

KEVIN DELGAUDIO

Mortgage Qualification
Made Easy

Disclaimer: This chapter is presented solely for educational and entertainment purposes. The author, author's employer, and publisher are not offering it as legal, financial, accounting, or other professional services advice. While best efforts have been used in preparing this book, the author, author's employer, and publisher make no representations or warranties of any kind and assume no liability of any kind with respect to the accuracy or completeness of the contents and specifically disclaim any implied warranties of merchantability or fitness of use for a particular purpose. Neither the author, author's employer, nor the publisher shall be held liable or responsible to any person or entity with respect to any loss or incidental or consequential damages caused, or alleged to have been caused, directly or indirectly, by the information or programs contained herein. No warranty may be created or extended by sales representatives or written sales materials. Every individual's situation is different, and the advice and strategies contained herein may not be suitable for your personal situation. You should seek the services of a competent professional before beginning any financial risk. The opinions contained within this chapter are the personal opinions of Kevin DelGaudio and are not the opinions of his employer, Jet Direct Mortgage.

Conversation with Kevin DelGaudio

Tell us about how you are helping your clients:

Kevin DelGaudio: Shortly after entering the real estate world, I noticed that most people went about purchasing a home in the wrong order. Most families would start looking for a home online or in a local real estate publication, then find an agent who would take them around to begin looking at these particular homes. It wasn't until they found a home they fell in love with that they would start considering the financial side of things – mainly qualifying for a mortgage.

Here is the big problem...almost everyone has an "issue" or "blemish" that may hamper them from immediately qualifying for a mortgage. Very few people have Perfect Credit, Perfect Income History, an abundance of cash for a down payment, and a low Debt to Income Ratio. Probably less than 5% of people are considered to be "plain vanilla" applicants, meaning that these people should easily qualify for a mortgage based upon their near perfect circumstances (those listed above).

Unfortunately, I have seen that this is not the case for very many people. I have found that most people have at least one "issue" that may hinder their qualifying for a mortgage for the home of their dreams. Here are some examples of why people may not qualify for the home they have their heart set on:

· Their down payment and income won't qualify them for such an expensive home
· Their credit score(s) is actually lower than they estimated
· There is an error(s) on their credit report
· There is a lien(s) on their credit report
· Their Debt to Income ratio is too high
· The appraisal is lower than expected

These are just a few of the many problems a potential borrower may unknowingly face.

Here is the problem: You find the home of your dreams, you apply for a mortgage and get denied, and lose the opportunity to purchase the home. Your family's hopes and dreams are destroyed, and the real estate agent loses a deal, doesn't get paid, and no longer wants to work with you...everyone loses!

Can this be avoided?

Yes, most of the time – with a little planning...Mortgage Planning!

Having worked for one of the major retail banks (one of the ones that got fined millions of dollars after the housing crisis of 2008), I honestly think that they preferred customers looking for a mortgage AFTER finding a home. In fact, until not so long ago, most Realtors® didn't even require a Prequalification letter from a mortgage lender before showing a house to prospective buyers. In the past, Real Estate agents would take buyers around, show them dozens of homes and when they finally found one, the deal would fall apart because the borrowers didn't qualify for the mortgage. Do you see why I feel the process is backwards?!

Doesn't it make much more sense to find out how much home you can afford and *IF* you can qualify, before you start shopping around for a home that you don't even know you can afford? Realtors® finally wised up and got tired of losing deals from prospective buyers who couldn't qualify for a mortgage. Today, most real estate agents will not even take you around, showing you houses unless you are Prequalified or Preapproved. This is much better, but still not quite as efficient as planning ahead – which is what I excel at.

What are the advantages of working with you versus any other option?

Kevin DelGaudio: I love the quote, "HOPE IS NOT A STRATEGY"
which is from a *US Air Force Special Ops Pilot*

The biggest advantage of working with me and utilizing my Mortgage Planning services is you get to find out what your particular problems and pitfalls are, in advance; so you can fix them or avoid them prior to actually applying for your mortgage. This prevents your entire family from feeling dejected when the home they fell in love with cannot be purchased because of failing to plan ahead. I am a Certified Mortgage Planning Specialist® (CMPS), a certification that the top 1% of Mortgage Loan Originators have obtained through focused and ongoing training. In addition to being better prepared to qualify for your mortgage, mortgage planning helps you decide which is the total lowest cost mortgage plan for your unique situation. No two mortgage situations are exactly the same and therefore each mortgage needs to be addressed individually – and you clearly can't do that by just picking the lowest rate!

Unfortunately, the vast majority of mortgage loan originators don't really dive in deep enough into your circumstances and work with you to decide which is the best mortgage option for you, not just which is the lowest rate. Sometimes the lowest rate can cost you far more as a total cost than a higher rate that is more in tune to your needs. This is why it is crucial to deal with a mortgage planner, and hopefully a Certified Mortgage Planning Specialist. When you work with me, I don't just present you with the lowest rate option. There are many factors that go into the total cost of your mortgage, and I address all of them. Let's look at an example:

Bob & Bill both buy an identical house on the same block at the same time and for the same price. Bob intends to stay there for the rest of his life, hopefully at least 30 years, so he can pay off the mortgage. Bill, on the other hand, knows he and his family are moving to another state within the next 2 to 3 years because of a pending promotion.

Do you think they should both take out the exact same mortgage?

Bob intends to spend thousands to "buy down" his interest rate, thereby lowering his total interest expense over the next 30 years. Do you believe that Bill would reap the same benefits, knowing he will be selling the house and paying off the mortgage within the next 3 years? Obviously not... buying down the interest rate would be a waste of money for Bill, as he would be long gone before he could reap the true benefits of a lower interest rate. I hope you are starting to see the bigger picture here...proper planning can make an astronomical difference in the total cost of your mortgage, but you must plan in advance with an experienced mortgage planner. The most important financial factor affecting your mortgage is the Total Cost, not the Lowest Rate. Contrary to conventional wisdom, many times the lower rate is the more expensive option.

*What do you feel are the biggest myths out there
when it comes to funding a home?*

Kevin DelGaudio: The biggest myth out there today is
that you need to pay off your mortgage as quickly as possible.
There are many plans to achieve this: biweekly mortgage
payments, making an extra payment at the end of the year,
putting your Christmas bonus and/or tax refund towards
your mortgage, choosing a shorter term than 30 years, etc.
This was a formula passed down from generations, dating
back to the Great Depression. At the time of the Depression,
banks had the right to call a loan due (request the loan be
paid off immediately) for any reason. This usually wasn't the
case, but as the Depression grew, banks had no cash on hand
and were forced to call many mortgages due. The result was
that most people lost their homes as they had no way to
cover their mortgage, let alone get a new one. That is
Depression Era thinking. The due on call clause is no longer
part of a mortgage contract. Just about the only way a lender
can "call" a mortgage due today, is by failure to pay as agreed
(Foreclosure). Again, I will illustrate by example.

Bob & Bill both buy a home whose cost and value are
identical, let's say $450,000.

Bob & Bill both have $150,000 in cash to put down on the
home. Bob puts his entire savings of $150,000 down on the
home, leaving a mortgage of $300,000. Bill, on the other
hand, spoke with a mortgage planner who explained to him
why it is best not to put so much cash into your home. Bill
went with an FHA loan and put down the minimum 3.5%, or
$15,750, leaving him with $134,250 in cash and a mortgage
balance of $434,250.

Let's look at some details. We are going to go with a 5%
interest rate and a 30-year term to keep things simple.

	BOB	BILL
Purchase Price	$450,000	$450,000
Down Payment	$150,000	$15,750
Cash On Hand Left Over	$0	$134,250
Mortgage Balance	$300,000	$434,250
Monthly Mortgage Payment	$1,250.00	$1,809.38

Bob's Advantages

Lower monthly mortgage payment (-$559.38)
Higher % of Home Equity
Lower % Mortgage Balance

Bill's Advantages

Higher tax deduction for mortgage payment (+$559.38)
$134,250 cash on hand for investment or emergency

The Ugly, But All Too Common, Scenario:

So far it looks like Bob is the smarter one here, even if only by a little...but wait!
Bob & Bill both walk into work on Monday and get fired.

Bob's Situation

·   Bob has no income to pay his monthly bills or his mortgage payment.
·   Bob cannot refinance his mortgage because he has no income.
·   Bob has $150,000 in cash trapped in his home that he can't access.
·   Bob has virtually no way to make ends meet.
·   After 90 days the banks will begin to foreclose on Bob's home.

Bill's Situation

·   Bill has no income to pay his monthly bills or his mortgage payment.
·   Bill cannot refinance his mortgage because he has no income.
·   Bill only has $15,750 in cash trapped in his home that he can't access.
·   Bill can survive for a couple of years with the cash he has in the bank.
·   Bill will be able to remain in his home because of proper planning and strategy.

Do you see why Proper Planning is so important?

It's NOT just about the rate!

What are some of the most common fears about funding a home?

Kevin DelGaudio: The most common fear is a borrower being concerned that they won't "qualify" for their mortgage. The problem is that most people don't even know what they need in order to qualify, until it is too late. I have seen time and again borrowers that were denied for a mortgage that would have easily qualified if they had spoken to a competent mortgage planner earlier in the process. While I do not have actual data figures, I would venture a guess that almost 75% of borrowers who were denied a mortgage could have been approved with proper and early planning.

Here is the real problem – the big retail banks and internet lenders don't want you to know the rules in advance. They want you to apply blindly, and if you are a "plain vanilla" borrower, they would love to approve you and have you for a customer. If you are in the vast majority who are not "plain vanilla", they don't want you "gaming" the system. When I talk about "gaming" the system, I am referring to knowing all the ins and outs that make getting approved more likely. Have you ever been told by a banker what your Debt to Income ratio needs to be? Probably not. When I worked for one of the big 3 retail banks, I was forbidden to tell my prospective clients any of the "game rules" , as well as not being able to tell them specifically why they were denied (Debt to Income ratio, Credit Score, low appraisal, etc.). In addition, because of all the wonderful new anti-discrimination legislation, I wasn't even allowed to tell a client upfront that they could not be approved based on their financial situation. This would be considered discrimination. That's right...if you walked into my office and wanted to apply for a mortgage but didn't even have a job or source of income, I was not allowed to tell you that you wouldn't be approved. I had to take your application anyway – knowing full well you would be denied. It doesn't seem like discrimination to me... just good old-fashioned common sense.

How can clients get past these fears?

Kevin DelGaudio: The way to get past these fears is to speak with a qualified mortgage planner as early in the home buying process as possible, well before you meet with a Realtor®. You want to confidently know how much home you can afford BEFORE you go home shopping... not AFTER!

When I first meet with a client, I explain the process in detail, the different scenarios they could take and how it will affect them in the short and long term. I spell out the negatives and positives for each scenario and work with the client until they fully understand and are comfortable moving forward with their game plan. We try and mitigate any and all possible glitches that may come up during the mortgage application approval process – and there are many. I make sure they understand as much as possible so they can truly make an intelligent and informed decision.

What other perceived obstacles do you see that might be preventing home buyers from seeking the help of a mortgage loan officer?

Kevin DelGaudio : Too many people get caught up on the closing costs and the rates. While nobody wants to pay more, you need to be comparing apples to apples, not oranges. Let me be very clear... no one is funding your loan for free. Mortgage lenders get paid either buy 1) Origination fees or 2) Interest Rate discounts – or a combination of both. Your main concern should be your Total Cost over the life of the mortgage. Food for thought: The average life of a mortgage in the United States is historically between 5 & 7 years, not 30 years. But most people don't know that, and the bankers certainly won't tell you that. Everything they discuss with you is all based on you keeping that mortgage for 30 years - I think that's crazy thinking and very poor planning!

What are some of the little-known pitfalls or common mistakes you see home buyers make on the road to funding a home and how can these be avoided?

Kevin DelGaudio: Not educating themselves before submitting an application. There is an old saying: "You can't win the game, if you don't know the rules". Again, start the mortgage education and application process early! If you are working with a competent mortgage professional, they will explain the application criteria and process in detail, before they take and submit your application.

TALE OF CAUTION

This is one of the very first tales of caution I ever learned in this business.

There was a hot shot Wall Street guy who was in his late twenties, making tons of money, and spending it just as fast. He wanted to buy a luxury condo in NYC. He met with his loan officer, took care of the paperwork, and scheduled a closing date. He spontaneously decided to take a quick vacation with his girlfriend to the Caribbean. He called his loan officer and informed him of the vacation and was assured everything was in place for the closing in 2 weeks. The client went away with his girlfriend and while away decided to propose to her... she accepted. Two days before closing, the Wall Street executive gets a disturbing call from his mortgage lender. "Michael, I have some bad news, the bank just ran your credit report again, and now your debt to income ratio is beyond the acceptable limits and the loan is being denied, so sorry."

What happened?

Unfortunately, Michael liked to spend it as fast as he made it. While on vacation he spent about $20,000 on the engagement ring and charged it on his credit card. This huge expenditure sent his debt to income ratio skyrocketing to an unacceptable level. The loan was denied, and the closing was cancelled. Apparently, the loan officer didn't explain things completely to Michael. Knowing his spending habits, if Michael were my client, I would have instructed him not to make any large expenditures until after the closing. The last I heard was that Michael refused to continue working with the original loan officer.

These pitfalls can simply be avoided by working with a competent loan officer, preferably one who specializes in mortgage planning. I cannot emphasize enough how important it is to plan in advance – remember probably 75% of denials could be approvals if the proper planning was conducted.

Can you share an example of how you have helped your clients overcome obstacles and succeed in funding a home?

Kevin DelGaudio: There are countless stories, but I will share a few that have stood out over the course of my career.

First, there was a young man I worked with who had the same name as his father. When his credit report came in, it had all of his debt and his father's mortgage on it. Had he gone shopping for a home first, the deal would have come to a dead halt as soon as we got the credit report back. Instead, he had come to me first – we were able to get his credit report corrected quickly and he was able to go home shopping with the confidence he would be approved. He did, and he was.

Secondly, I worked with a young couple years ago who were both the caretakers of their aging parents. To make it easy on them, they would pay all of their parents' debts and expenses from their personal accounts. There was so much co-mingling of money in and out of different accounts it was almost impossible to keep track of. This is something any mortgage lender would have scrutinized to no end. I explained that the banks like to see a minimum of 3 months bank statements, and that they needed to clean up and consolidate the way they handled their parents' finances. I had them set up separate accounts for their parents and stop making payments from and deposits into their own personal accounts. Their parents' finances were now separated, and their personal finances now only showed *their* income and *their* expenses. After four months they started looking for a home and found one relatively quickly. Their mortgage application was quickly approved since the finances showed solely their activity.

I already shared the infamous story about the Wall Street guy who bought an expensive engagement ring just before his closing. Yes, the banks pull your credit just before closing to make sure nothing drastic has changed. This is a scenario that everyone can learn from.

Lastly, there was another very young couple who were renting an apartment in a not so nice area and wanted to buy a home and start a family. After meeting with me, we came to the conclusion that they couldn't afford a home in the area they had their hearts set on. Unfortunately, their Debt to Income ratio was too high (they had a lot of personal debt), even for the least expensive homes in the area. Needless to say, they were heartbroken as it destroyed their dream of starting a family. I suggested that either one of them get a part time job and start paying down as much of their debt as possible. This would lower their debt and raise their income. They were excited, and they both went out and got part time second jobs. Within 9 months, they had paid down so much debt (this couple was so determined) that they were now able to easily qualify for some of the lower priced homes in the area. Within a year, they bought their new home and immediately started a family. The wife left her 2nd job while he kept his and they promised me they would be saving towards a larger home for the very near future. You guessed it... less than two years later, they did just that.

...and so can you!

What inspired you to become a Mortgage Loan Officer?

Kevin DelGaudio: I got the bug to enter the mortgage business back when I was a real estate agent (why I did that is a long story for another time). I will tell you something about me: I have always been and fought for the underdog. I can't stand idly by and watch injustice. In addition, I have a great knack for finding out what I don't know. While I was a real estate agent, I watched deal after deal fall through for the same reasons you've been reading about above. Day after day, prospective home buyers would shop for a house, find one, apply for a mortgage, get denied, and the deal was lost. Not a great way to make money! I spoke with many other real estate agents who complained of the same thing. One day an old timer gave me this advice: "Get used to it, it's just the way this business is. Deals fall apart every single day, trust me, you're not going to change it, just get used to it."

That's all I needed to hear...I was now on a mission to do just that – Change Things!

I spoke to a childhood friend of mine whose neighbor was a longtime mortgage broker. We met and spoke about the industry and what it took to become a mortgage loan officer. This was just before they made education and licensing mandatory (and from the war stories I had heard, it wasn't soon enough). I dug in and read everything I could find on the mortgage industry – history, trends, the underwriting process and criteria, etc. I got licensed and jumped in with both feet. I would like to say it was easy sailing in the beginning, but it wasn't. People still came to me AFTER they found a home, and AFTER it was too late to correct any issues that would prevent them from being approved.

I am on a one-man mission to reverse the home buyer borrower's process...

OLD WAY			
Start looking for a home	Meet with Real Estate Agent	Meet with Mortgage Loan Officer	Apply for a mortgage - Hope & Pray

RIGHT WAY			
Meet with Mortgage Loan Officer	Start looking for a home	Meet with Real Estate Agent	Apply for a mortgage with Confidence

Can you share a lesson you learned early on, that still impacts how you do business today?

Kevin DelGaudio: Never rely on word of mouth for what is on a Credit Report. You may believe you have perfect credit (and you may deserve it), but unfortunately there are mistakes on Credit Reports. You don't know what is on your Credit Report unless you have actually READ your Credit Report. Mistakes happen all the time. There are dozens of mistakes; another family member's info, outdated info, incorrect info, etc., etc., the list goes on. When I have clients who are wise enough to start their home buying process with me, before they go house hunting, I suggest they go online and purchase a Three Bureau Credit Report. This solves three issues: 1) We can see what is actually showing on their Credit Report and can plug that information into the qualifying formula, 2) because the credit was pulled by the consumer, it will not affect their credit rating, and 3) if there are any errors or discrepancies, we can address and resolve them before a mortgage application is submitted. The Credit Report is the great unknown. We need to see/know what is actually on the report to make an intelligent decision regarding the approval process. More surprises have come from Credit Reports than I care to remember.

What's the most important question home buyers should ask themselves as they consider funding a home?

Kevin DelGaudio: Am I fully prepared and ready to apply for a mortgage at this time, so that I have an excellent chance of being approved under my current financial situation? Unfortunately, only a competent licensed Mortgage Loan Originator can answer that for you... make sure you choose your loan officer wisely!

What's the most important thing home buyers should consider when evaluating a Mortgage Loan Officer?

Kevin DelGaudio: I call it the choice between Rate & Advice. If you are looking at just the rate, then there are thousands of loan officers who could help you. It doesn't matter how qualified they are, they are just order takers. "Oh, you want a mortgage, here is our rate". Unfortunately, there is so much more to the process, and most prospective borrowers don't find out until it's too late. Have you ever heard a friend, co-worker, or family member complain about how bad their mortgage broker was? If so, then they hired someone as described above – a rate quoter. It's all about getting your application, so the next guy/gal doesn't, then they hope that you will be approved. It's like a real estate agent telling you that they can get you more money than your house is worth if you just sign the listing agreement – it's all about getting you to sign the contract, so the next guy/gal won't. It's simply not true.

You are never going to get more than your house is worth and it's the same with mortgage rates. Too many mortgage loan officers tease prospective borrowers with low rates (and usually hidden fees) before they even know your financial circumstances. There are numerous factors that go into pricing a mortgage and getting an accurate rate. If you get a mortgage rate BEFORE you give all your financial information and the entire details of the transaction, you are getting a "Quoted Rate." There is an exceptionally high chance your final rate will be higher.

You want "Actual Rates"!

A quoted rate is a rate based on assumptions (and you know what happens when you assume) and is rarely the final rate that is eventually given if the mortgage is approved. Take a guess whether the final rate you'll receive is higher or lower than the "Quoted Rate" ... You guessed it...almost always higher.

An "Actual Rate" is based on all the factors of a transaction, so the final rate is usually the same. It can differ slightly based on final circumstances and numbers, but is usually quite accurate.

QUOTED RATE = GUESSING AND LOW BALLING
ACTUAL RATE = CAREFULLY CALCULATED ESTIMATE BASED ON FACTS

Which rate would you prefer?

Which leads me to the most important question when choosing your mortgage loan officer, 'Do you want rate or advice?' "Rate" means they are just going to shop the best rate for you, regardless of the fees and overall or total cost of the mortgage. "Advice" means they are going to scrutinize every option available to you, given your unique circumstances and desires and present multiple options with different rates, terms, fees, and total cost of the loan.

Please remember the examples from earlier in this chapter. Everyone's situation and circumstances are unique and different. The "Rate" approach is a cookie cutter approach that is forced upon everyone but works out well for very few. The "Advice" approach is really the only good option because it takes your unique situation into account and provides the best alternatives based on those unique factors. It is customized to your personal situation, and that always is the best solution.

How can someone find out more about you and how you can help?

Kevin DelGaudio: The best way to contact me is via cell phone or text at 917-204-4701 or email at Kevin@TheCertifiedMortgagePlanner.com. I usually respond within 1 hour or less.

SPECIAL FREE OFFER

I am putting together a Special Report for all of the readers of this book. It is titled: "Home Buying Insights – Insider Secrets to Mortgage Approval" and it is a quick but comprehensive guide that goes over the basics of what is required to get approved for a mortgage in today's market. Simply send an email to: Report@TheCertifiedMortgagePlanner.com and I will forward you a FREE copy.

Please remember that currently I am only licensed to conduct business in the states of: New York & New Jersey, but my mortgage bank – Jet Direct Mortgage - is licensed in multiple states and I can put you in contact with a licensed loan officer within the company for your particular state.

Jet Direct Mortgage is currently licensed in these states: Alabama, California, Colorado, Connecticut, Florida, Georgia, Maine, Maryland, Michigan, New Jersey, New York, North Carolina, Ohio, Pennsylvania, South Carolina, Tennessee, and Virginia.

If you have questions or concerns, please do not hesitate to reach out to me. If I can't personally help, I will try and point you in the right direction. Good luck with your home buying! I hope this book, and especially this chapter, has helped you.

KEVIN DELGAUDIO, CMPS

Certified Mortgage Planning Specialist®
Mortgage Loan Originator, NMLS # 303722
Jet Direct Mortgage NMLS # 3542

Kevin DelGaudio was a Real Estate agent before becoming a mortgage loan officer and unfortunately, he had heard about and personally encountered so many "lost deals"; because too many prospective homeowners didn't speak to a loan officer before shopping for their home. They would go shop for a home, find one they loved, go apply for a mortgage, and many times get denied – because they weren't properly prepared. Eventually, he grew so frustrated, he gave up working in real estate to pursue a career in Mortgage Banking. He first got into the mortgage business after the major real estate collapse of 2007 – 2008, right around the time they started requiring mandatory licensing of all Mortgage Loan Officers.

Everyone's personal and financial circumstances are different and need to be addressed on an individual basis, not some cookie cutter formula to qualify you for a loan (the way over 90% of loan officers today operate). Most importantly, they need to be addressed BEFORE the mortgage application process begins. Always on the side of the underdog, Kevin tries to get to as many prospective home buyers as possible before they go home shopping. Unfortunately, the market was designed the opposite way: first find a home then go for a mortgage – nothing could be more wrong in his opinion.

Finally, Kevin decided that he was going to make reversing the mortgage application and home buying process a personal mission of his – a one-man crusade to help more home buyers through the correct process by planning ahead for their home purchase.

Today Kevin is a Certified Mortgage Planning Specialist - CMPS® which is a certification held by the top 1% of mortgage professionals; who are like minded and see the planning process as the most important aspect of the home buying process. "Planning ahead is by far the most important way to greatly improve your chances of getting approved for a mortgage – let me help you do just that!

WEBSITE: www.TheCertifiedMortgagePlanner.com

EMAIL: Kevin@TheCertifiedMortgagePlanner.com

LINKEDIN:

www.linkedin.com/company/TheCertifiedMortgagePlanner

FACEBOOK: The Certified Mortgage Planner

TWITTER: https://twitter.com/TheCertifiedMLO

CELL: 917-204-4701

OFFICE: 631-574-1306 Ext 5552

FAX: 888-677-6074

ABOUT THE PUBLISHER

Mark Imperial is a Best-Selling Author, Syndicated Business Columnist, Syndicated Radio Host, and internationally recognized Stage, Screen, and Radio Host of numerous business shows spotlighting leading experts, entrepreneurs, and business celebrities.

His passion is discovering noteworthy business owners, professionals, experts, and leaders who do great work, and sharing their stories and secrets to their success with the world on his syndicated radio program titled "Remarkable Radio".

Mark is also the media marketing strategist and voice for some of the world's most famous brands. You can hear his voice over the airwaves weekly on Chicago radio and worldwide on iHeart Radio.

Mark is a Karate black belt, teaches kickboxing, loves Thai food, House Music, and his favorite TV shows are infomercials.

Learn more:
www.MarkImperial.com
www.ImperialAction.com
www.RemarkableRadioShow.com